EXTRAORDINARY
WOMEN *WITH* CAMERAS

EXTRAORDINARY
WOMEN WITH
CAMERAS

35 Photographers Who Changed
How We See the World

WRITTEN BY
DARCY REED

ILLUSTRATED BY
VANESSA PEREZ

rockynook

Extraordinary Women with Cameras:
35 Photographers Who Changed How We See the World
Darcy Reed

Editor: Kelly Reed
Project manager: Lisa Brazieal
Marketing coordinator: Katie Walker
Copyeditor: Chelsea Tornetto
Design: Frances Baca
Cover illustrations: Vanessa Perez

ISBN: 978-1-68198-879-5
1st Edition (1st printing, September 2022)
© 2022 Darcy Reed
All illustrations © Vanessa Perez

Rocky Nook Inc.
1010 B Street, Suite 350
San Rafael, CA 94901
USA
www.rockynook.com

Distributed in the UK and Europe by Publishers Group UK
Distributed in the U.S. and all other territories by Ingram Publisher Services

Library of Congress Control Number: 2022937110

This book is printed on acid-free paper.
Printed in China

CONTENTS

INTRODUCTION

Ever since photography was invented almost 200 years ago, women all over the world have taken groundbreaking, inspiring photographs. In this book you'll explore the stories of 35 of the most talented historical and contemporary shutterbugs! Some of their names may be familiar, and some may be totally new, but all of them contributed to the fascinating, beautiful field of photography.

If you've ever snapped a selfie or posed your friends for a group shot, you're following in the footsteps of these truly extraordinary women! So, we've included some fun photo ideas for you to try and new photography terms for you to learn. We hope this book inspires you to pick up your own camera and start snapping interesting photos. Who knows? Maybe your work will be featured in a museum or book one day!

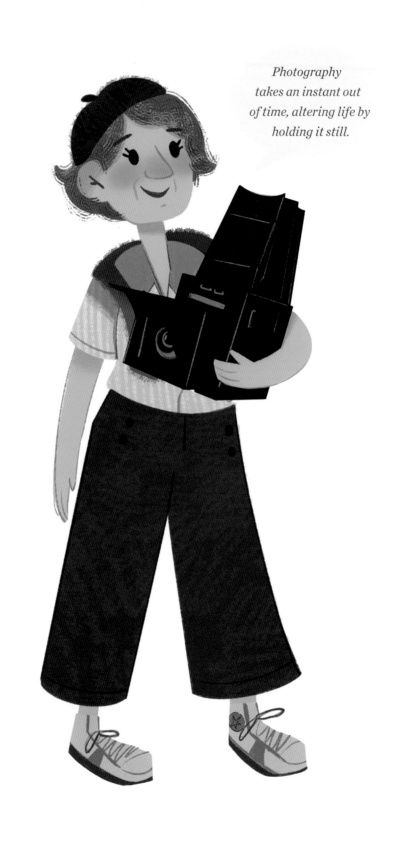

Photography takes an instant out of time, altering life by holding it still.

DOROTHEA LANGE

Finding Beauty in Tragedy

1895 to 1965

Have you ever had a moment in your life that you just HAD to capture on camera? A moment that you wanted to make sure you remembered forever? Dorothea Lange did too! But Dorothea wasn't capturing happy memories like birthday parties or selfies with friends. She used her photography skills to record some of history's most tragic moments. Her photos of the Dust Bowl during the Great Depression and prisoners in Japanese internment camps during World War II made sure Americans would never forget those tragedies.

We have to make room for other people. It's a wheel—you get on, you go to the end, and someone else has the same opportunity to go to the end, and so on, and somebody else takes their place.

VIVIAN MAIER
Secret Photographer

1926 TO 2009

No one suspected Vivian Maier was a photographer. They thought she was just a nanny! But during the 1950s and 1960s Vivian took thousands of photos of people, buildings, and activities in Chicago and New York. She hid them away in huge suitcases, and they were only discovered after her death, by a photographer who bought them at an auction. Her sneaky but stunning street photography continues to inspire.

? **What is street photography?** *Have you ever taken a snapshot of a stranger's outfit or a random building because it looked cool? That's street photography! Capturing a candid moment that might otherwise be unnoticed is a hallmark of the genre.*

→ **Your Turn!** *Next time you're out in a city and you see an interesting piece of architecture or a stranger with a unique sense of style, snap a street photograph inspired by Vivian!*

*Photography
is actually a wonderful
medium for a young person
to just go out and discover
themselves and discover the
world around them.*

ANNIE LEIBOVITZ

Photographer of the Stars

1949 TO TODAY

Annie Leibovitz started as a photographer for *Rolling Stone* magazine in the 1970s and has photographed some of the most famous people in the world, including President Barack Obama, John Lennon, and Queen Elizabeth! While she's known for her dramatic portraits, she has also shot playful and fun images like a Disney-themed series with Taylor Swift as Rapunzel and Scarlett Johansson as Cinderella. Her iconic photos have been featured in magazines like *Vogue* and *Vanity Fair* and she has taken portraits of so many celebrities that she's become a celebrity herself!

*I didn't really think
about being the first woman...
I just go for things regardless of the
boundaries because I've always
had to break boundaries.*

MING SMITH

Breaking Boundaries

1947 TO TODAY

Ming Smith studied microbiology at Howard University then moved to New York City where she worked as a model and pursued her love of photography. In the 1970s she became the first Black woman whose photography was acquired by the Museum of Modern Art in New York City. She was also the first female member of the Kamoinge Workshop, an exclusive club of Black photographers. She has photographed many celebrities, such as Tina Turner, Grace Jones, Nina Simone, and James Baldwin, as well as many inspiring images of everyday people.

*Collective joy
around the world is what
we all need right now.*

ANNE GEDDES

Baby Whisperer

1956 TO **TODAY**

Babies, with their chubby cheeks and tiny toes, are probably some of the most photographed people on the planet! And while they're cute no matter what, Anne Geddes is famous for her ability to capture them at their very cutest! Books of her creative baby photos have sold millions of copies around the world, and she still takes baby portraits today. Her images can be found on calendars, journals, greeting cards, and baby books, and they're guaranteed to make you say, "Awwww!"

Saturate yourself with your subject, and the camera will all but take you by the hand and point the way.

MARGARET BOURKE-WHITE

Woman of Many Firsts

1904 TO 1971

Margaret Bourke-White broke barriers as the first woman to do many notable things. In 1930, while on assignment with *Fortune* magazine, she was the first Westerner allowed to take photographs in the Soviet Union. She was later hired as the first female photographer at *LIFE* magazine, where she became the first female war correspondent and the first woman allowed in combat zones during WWII. She also photographed the devastating effects of the Great Depression.

What is photojournalism? *When photos are used to tell the story of a historic or current event, that's photojournalism. Photojournalists have used pictures to tell the stories of wars, political movements, and even the construction of famous buildings!*

Your Turn! *The next time there is an important event in your community, document it by taking pictures! What shots will you need to capture to help others understand what happened?*

Photography as a medium has amazing potential.

KUNIÉ SUGIURA

No Camera Required

Kunié Sugiura is a Japanese painter and photographer who is known for creating striking images of abstract shapes, flowers, and creatures. Her preferred medium is called a photogram, which captures silhouettes of people and objects, and is sometimes called "camera-less photography."

What is a photogram? *You don't always need a camera to take a photo! A photogram is made by placing an object directly onto or in front of light-sensitive material (such as photographic paper) while in the dark, and then exposing it to bright light to create an image.*

I really believe there are things nobody would see if I didn't photograph them.

DIANE ARBUS

Friend to Outsiders

1923 to 1971

Diane Arbus celebrated people who were different and used her photos to capture their unique beauty. Though her photos were black–and-white, her subjects—including circus performers, twins, and ordinary people on the streets of New York—are colorful and captivating. Her ground-breaking images made her one of the most influential photographers of all time.

 Your Turn! *Use the filters on your phone or computer to change some of your photos to black and white. How does it change the mood of the images?*

*If a photographer
cares about the people before
the lens and is compassionate, much
is given. It is the photographer,
not the camera, that is the
instrument.*

EVE ARNOLD

The Compassionate Photographer

1912 TO 2012

Eve Arnold was one of nine children born to immigrant Russian parents and it seemed unlikely she would ever become a world-famous photographer. She first attended medical school but after getting a camera as a present from her boyfriend, her love of photography blossomed. In 1957 she became the first woman to join the Magnum photo agency (an exclusive club of big-name photographers) and traveled the world taking stunning photos of people from all walks of life, from famous celebrities to ordinary working-class people. She was known for her empathy for her subjects, whether they were celebrities like Marilyn Monroe (whom she became friends with), civil rights activists including Malcolm X, or everyday people such as migrant workers.

*It's just me and a
mirror and a camera and a
backdrop, and that's about it. I've
always felt that I'm able to be a little
more experimental because no one is
around if it doesn't go well.*

CINDY SHERMAN

Selfie Chameleon

1954 ᴛᴏ TODAY

Famous for her creative self-portraits, Cindy Sherman uses imaginative makeup and costumes and a mirror to put herself in front of the camera. Her unique and daring images have inspired many other artists.

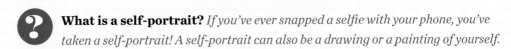 **What is a self-portrait?** *If you've ever snapped a selfie with your phone, you've taken a self-portrait! A self-portrait can also be a drawing or a painting of yourself.*

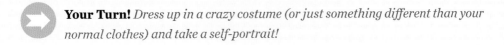 **Your Turn!** *Dress up in a crazy costume (or just something different than your normal clothes) and take a self-portrait!*

FLORESTINE PERRAULT COLLINS

Entrepreneur in the Big Easy

1895 ᴛᴏ 1988

In the 1920s through the 1940s Florestine Perrault Collins was one of the few Black women who made a living as a photographer in America. She opened her own studio in New Orleans and used her skills to capture snapshots of African American life in the early 20th century, including everyday events like graduations and celebrations. Her photography business allowed her to support her family through the Great Depression and her art is known for reflecting the "pride, elegance, and dignity" of her subjects.

Your Turn! *The next time your family celebrates a wedding, graduation, or birthday, document it with pictures! Maybe someday others will look back at your snapshots of "21st century life."*

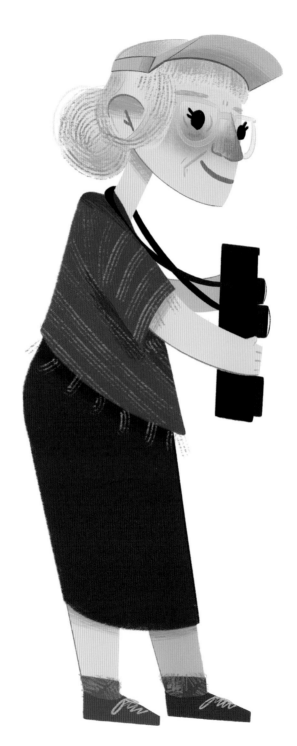

Which of my photographs is my favorite? The one I'm going to take tomorrow.

IMOGEN CUNNINGHAM

Grandmother of Photography

1883 ᴛᴏ 1976

One of the first professional female photographers in America, Imogen Cunningham took photos of people, industrial landscapes, and street scenes, but is best known for her botanical photography (close-up shots of plants and flowers). Throughout her career she explored lots of different types of photography, from taking pictures of flowers to photographing celebrities for *Vanity Fair*! She has been called the "Grandmother of Photography" for helping photography become recognized as a legitimate art form.

 Your Turn! *Go out to your yard or a nearby park and take close-up photos of plants and flowers. Try to discover new plants you've never noticed before!*

CHRISTINA BROOM

Accidental Photojournalist

1862 TO 1939

Christina Broom never planned to become a photographer. She only took up photography at the age of 40 to support her family after her husband was injured and became unable to work. She taught herself how to use a camera and sold her photos as postcards. But soon, she discovered a true passion for the work and became a professional photojournalist. Broom became close with the British royal family, taking photos of the king and queen. Her best-known photographs are of the suffragettes and the early feminist movement.

*Since I'm
inarticulate, I express
myself with images.*

HELEN LEVITT

Inspired by City Streets

1913 ᴛᴏ 2009

Helen Levitt spent over sixty years photographing candid shots of people and places in the streets of New York City, capturing playful and poetic glimpses of daily life. She was first inspired by chalk drawings done by children around the city, which became her first photo series. She made sure to include the children who drew the artwork in the photos.

SALLY MANN

Photographing the Familiar

1951 to TODAY

It's only natural to want to capture photos of the people and places we love most—and Sally Mann is no different. Though she is one of the most renowned photographers in America, having won numerous awards and published several books, Sally doesn't photograph celebrities or fashion icons. She's best known for her black-and-white portraits of her own children and striking landscape photos of the American South. In 2001 she was named "America's Best Photographer" by *Time* magazine!

 Your Turn! *Skip the staged photos of your brunch plate, and snap some pictures of the people you love the most! You'll be glad you did!*

I would rather take a photograph than be one.

LEE MILLER

Model Turned Photographer

1907 TO 1977

Lee Miller began her career as a fashion model in New York City in the 1920s after she was discovered on the street by legendary *Vogue* publisher Condé Nast. But after a while, she grew tired of being in front of a camera and decided to get behind one! She worked with famous artists Man Ray and Picasso in Paris and later became a war correspondent for *Vogue* in Europe during World War II, photographing major events like the London Blitz and the liberation of Paris.

The camera gave me an incredible freedom. It gave me the ability to parade through the world and look at people and things very, very closely.

CARRIE MAE WEEMS

The Multi-Talented Artist

1953 TO TODAY

For more than 30 years Carrie Mae Weems has used her extraordinary talents in multiple areas (photography, fabric art, digital images, audio, video, and text) to create groundbreaking artwork. One of her most famous projects was the "Kitchen Table Series," a collection of black-and-white photographs showing different family scenes taking place around a kitchen table. In 2014 she became the first Black woman to have a retrospective of her years of artwork displayed at the famous Guggenheim museum in New York City.

One thing LIFE *always taught us—they'd say film is cheap. Use it. Shoot, shoot, shoot.*

MARTHA HOLMES

The Career Photojournalist

1923 TO 2006

Martha Holmes's career began at the *Louisville Courier-Journal* and *The Louisville Times* newspapers. She was hired as a photography assistant but became a full-time photographer during WWII when most of the male photographers were serving in the military. She later worked for *LIFE* magazine and by 1950 was named one of the top 10 female photographers in America.

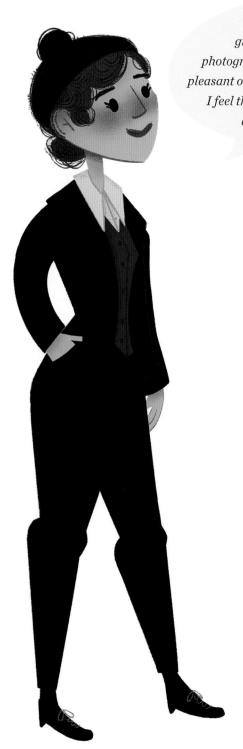

FRANCES BENJAMIN JOHNSTON

Business Builder

1864 TO 1952

Frances Benjamin Johnston was given her first camera by close family friend George Eastman, the founder of Kodak film. After working for the Eastman Kodak company for a few years, Johnston quickly established herself as a professional portrait photographer and opened her own studio in Washington D.C. Her clients included Susan B. Anthony and Mark Twain, as well as President Teddy Roosevelt and his family, among many others. Johnston encouraged other women to try photography too, writing "What a Woman Can Do with a Camera" for the *Ladies' Home Journal* in 1897.

The still image continues to have a ton of strength. An image taken out of context from one fraction of a second to the next can tell a story, and if photographers are looking to tell a certain story, they can curate those slices of time to their advantage.

JILL GREENBERG

The Master Digital Manipulator

1967 TO TODAY

If you've ever browsed the covers of magazines in the checkout line at the grocery store, you've probably seen Jill Greenberg's work! She has made stylized, distinctive portraits of famous people, including Gwen Stefani, Arnold Schwarzenegger, Paul Rudd, and Amy Schumer. She is credited with creating a distinctive new photography style using digital effects to create eye-popping photographs that look almost like paintings. Other photos she's known for include a series of portraits of monkeys and a controversial collection of pictures of children crying. Many photographers have since tried to copy her style, but she remains a groundbreaking original talent.

ANNA ATKINS

The Publishing Pioneer

1799 TO 1871

Anna Atkins was an artist, botanist (someone who studies plants), and photography pioneer. She was one of the first women to ever take photos! Her scientist father encouraged her to study plants, and she captured their images using cyanotype prints (similar to the photogram process described on page 21). Her book on plants is the first book ever published featuring photographic images!

The most important
skill of the photographer is to
know how to see... With just one click,
the lens captures the exterior world
at the same time it captures the
photographer's inner world.

GERMAINE KRULL

The World Traveler

1897 TO 1985

From the time she was born, Germaine Krull was a traveler. Born in East Prussia, she and her family moved to Bosnia, Paris, Slovenia, and rural Germany, before settling in Munich. As an adult, she became politically active, which at the time was very dangerous and even caused her to be arrested more than once! In the 1920s she settled in Paris where she photographed fashion models, everyday street scenes, and even fellow artists. She published one of the first books solely made up of photographs, called *Métal*. It was a collection of images of iron objects like bridges, cranes, and the Eiffel Tower, and it is considered by many to be one of the most important photo books in history. She traveled and took photos all over the world, including Brazil, Republic of the Congo, Southeast Asia (where she managed a hotel), and India (where she lived with Tibetan monks!).

*The most magical
experience of photography
is when it's in your hands, because
it's here—you're touching it,
you can hear it, you can
smell it.*

DAYANITA SINGH

Interactive Artist

1961 ᵀᴼ TODAY

Dayanita Singh's photographs are known for capturing beautiful glimpses of Indian culture and life, but the unique ways she displays her work are what REALLY make her stand out. Not content with simply hanging a photo on a gallery wall, she combines her love of books and photography to create totally unique art installations that allow people to walk around, explore, and even hold her art in their hands. Called "book objects" or "pocket museums," Singh's art defies stuffy rules and makes viewing her photos interactive and fun.

 Your Turn! *Print out some of your favorite photographs and try to come up with creative ways to display them.*

ILSE BING

Queen of Leica

1899 TO 1998

Ilse Bing was dubbed the "Queen of Leica" for her skills using the Leica camera, a groundbreaking small-format camera that allowed users to photograph fast-moving events. She was largely self-taught and developed her own quirky signature style, with often sharp angles, dizzying aerial shots, and blurred motion. This use of innovative and unusual techniques is referred to as "avant-garde" photography.

 Your Turn! *Try taking some avant-garde photos by shooting ordinary buildings and places at unexpected angles and views!*

I'm just interested in people on the edges. I feel an affinity for people who haven't had the best breaks in society. I'm always on their side.

MARY ELLEN MARK

Photographer of the Homeless and Hollywood Stars

1940 ᴛᴏ 2015

Mary Ellen Mark's photography captured the lives of both the successful and the struggling. She took pictures of people living on the fringes of society, including runaway homeless kids in Seattle, those living in poverty in India, and protestors of the Vietnam War. She also spent time on movie sets, where she captured behind-the-scenes moments of some of the most famous actors in the world. She published several books and a film about her work, and her photo essays and portraits were exhibited worldwide and appeared in many publications and museums. No matter where she went or who she photographed, she always tried to show their humanity and approach them with empathy.

You cannot see me from where I look at myself.

FRANCESCA WOODMAN

Creator of Haunting Self-Portraits

1958 TO 1981

Francesca Woodman is remembered for her innovation in photography by taking ghostly, beautiful self-portraits. Unlike other self-portraits, which provided a clear view of the subject's face, Woodman would often hide behind furniture or otherwise blur the photo by manipulating light, movement, and long exposure times.

*I earnestly advise
women of artistic tastes
to train for the
unworked field of modern
photography.*

GERTRUDE KÄSEBIER

The Fine Artist

1852 *TO* 1934

As a child, Gertrude Käsebier dreamed of creating pictures. She would even paint with water that spilled on the floor! After she was married and had three children, she was finally able to attend art school, where her love of painting gave way to a love of photography. She opened her own photography studio in New York City, which became a great success. She was known for her photos portraying motherhood and her portraits of Native Americans. She was also a founder of the group called Photo-Secession, which was made up of fellow photographers who championed pictorialism and photography as a fine art. In 1899 one of her photos sold for $100, at that time the highest price ever paid for a photograph! During a time when most photographers were men, Gertrude Käsebier passionately encouraged other women to become more involved in the art form.

What is pictorialism? *Pictorialism was a photography trend from about 1885 to 1915 where artists would manipulate their photos to create dreamier, more soft-focus images. Today we can change a photo using Instagram filters or Photoshop, but back then photographers had to develop photos by hand and manipulate them in darkrooms to create unusual effects.*

*I want to make believe
that our world is a little more
magical, a little bit more special,
than it actually is.*

DULCE PINZÓN

Chronicler of Everyday Superheroes

1974 to TODAY

Dulce Pinzón was named by *Forbes* as "One of the 50 most creative Mexicans in the world." Her iconic "The Real Story of the Superheroes" series featured several immigrant workers in New York City dressed as superheroes. Her goal was to highlight the invisible "superheroes" people encounter in everyday life. She wanted to "pay homage to these brave and determined men and women that somehow manage, without the help of any supernatural power, to withstand extreme conditions of labor in order to help their families and communities survive and prosper." She currently lives in Brooklyn and her works can be found in museums all over the world.

 Your Turn! *Take a photo of someone you think is an everyday superhero and share it with them!*

*If your pictures
aren't good enough,
you're not close enough.*

This quote is often attributed to
Robert Capa, but many believe it was
actually Taro who said it.

GERDA TARO

The Brave War Photographer

1910 ᴛᴏ 1937

Gerda Taro and her partner, Robert Capa, were actually born as Gerta Pohorylle and Endre Friedmann. They both adopted aliases to escape political intolerance toward Jewish people in the 1930s. She courageously rode with soldiers to take photos of wartime conflict and, tragically, was the first woman who died doing this brave task while covering the Spanish Civil War. She was just 26 years old.

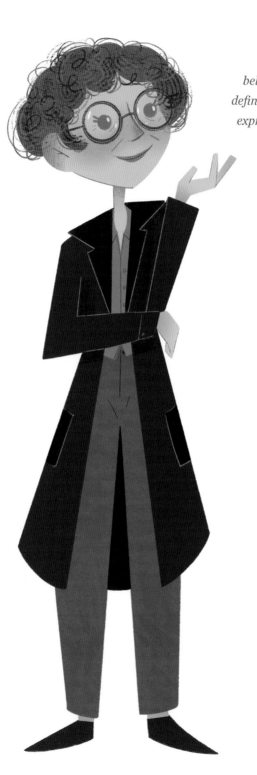

For me, photography is pure fiction... I don't believe that I am making any defined statement. Instead, I am expressing something, an echo of the world maybe.

SARAH MOON

The High Fashion Photographer

1941 TO TODAY

After a successful modeling career in France and England, Sarah Moon decided to take the camera into her own hands. She became known for her distinctive dreamy style and worked with many major fashion labels such as Chanel and Dior. In 1972 she became the first woman to shoot the Pirelli Calendar, an exclusive photography calendar that is still published today.

I took to photography
like a duck to water.
I never wanted to do
anything else.

BERENICE ABBOTT

Genius Inventor

1898 TO 1991

Berenice Abbott was not only a genius photographer but also an inventor. She discovered her love of photography while working in Paris and later moved to New York City where she documented the changing urban landscape. In 1937 her work was featured in a museum exhibition called "Changing New York." Her grand, dramatic photos of the bridges, skyscrapers, and streets being built during that time are legendary. She also invented photographic equipment and even held four patents on her inventions. Her creations included a distortion easel (a flexible easel designed to create interesting effects on photos), an autopole (an adjustable pole used for holding equipment), a cloth vest with many pockets, a candid camera, and more.

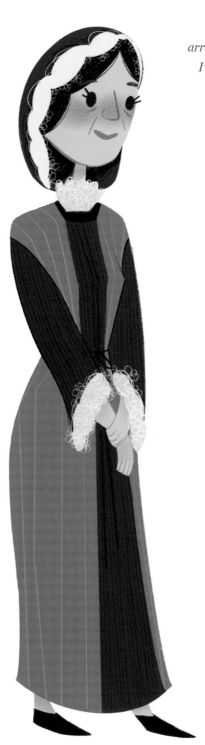

*Beauty, you're under
arrest. I have a camera, and
I'm not afraid to use it.*

JULIA MARGARET CAMERON

Embracing Flaws to Create Beauty

1815 TO 1879

Julia Margaret Cameron discovered photography later in life at the age of 48 when her daughter gave her a camera as a gift. Because of her notable position in Victorian English high society, she was able to photograph many legendary figures in her short career, including famous poet Alfred Tennyson and legendary naturalist Charles Darwin! She also took many portraits of her friends and family, whom she would often pose as religious or literary characters. Her mesmerizing portraits were considered impressive because of their dramatic soft-focus style, and the fact that she included imperfections such as scratches, streaks, and fingerprints, which made the photos unique.

*When you do
not like human beings,
you cannot make good
portraits.*

GISÈLE FREUND

The History Documentarian

1908 TO 2000

Gisèle Freund was born into a Jewish family in Germany and used documentary photography to record the rise of the Nazi party. She was an activist against the growing fascist movement but when it became too dangerous to remain in Germany she fled to France. She could only take her camera and photo negatives, which she bravely taped to her body to sneak past guards. In France she continued taking photos and became known for her portraits of artists and writers. She was the first woman in France to start using color film for her photos and was known for engaging her subjects in conversation to put them at ease, rather than formally posing them in a studio like most other photographers. She was known for her charm and ability to connect with people, which made her able to win over the confidence of the most difficult and camera-shy subjects.

? **What is documentary photography?** *Like photojournalism, documentary photography is the straightforward style of taking accurate photos of people, places, and historic events.*

I want imagination in
the photographs I take. It's like
a prologue. You wonder, "What's
going on?" You feel something
is going to happen.

RINKO KAWAUCHI

Making the Ordinary Extraordinary

1972 TO TODAY

Rinko Kawauchi is a Japanese photographer known for her dreamy, otherworldly photographs. She has published several photo books and her work is featured in museums all over the world. By using soft focus and lighting techniques, her photography is known for showing ordinary scenes in a brand-new light. According to an article in *Aperture* magazine, "in her images of keenly observed gestures and details, Kawauchi reveals the mysterious and beautiful realm at the edge of the everyday world."

*Just composing
the photograph, seeing it
instantly, and being ready to
document on the fly…
you have to have that
camera ready.*

COREEN SIMPSON

Photographer and Jewelry Designer

1942 ᴛᴏ TODAY

Coreen Simpson is an influential photographer and jewelry designer. She started her career as a photojournalist, covering events all over the world. Her photos have been featured in *Vogue, Essence, The New York Times*, and in many museums. In the 1990s she combined her love of photography with her love of fashion and started a jewelry collection known as the Black Cameo. In the Black Cameo, Simpson took the old tradition of cameo necklaces—where a side-silhouette of a person is the key feature—and featured portraits of Black women.

*If you'd like learn more about these extrodinary women
and see examples of their work be sure to visit the web site at this address
or scan the QR code below!*

HTTPS://ROCKYNOOK.COM/EXTRAORDINARYWOMEN/

FURTHER EXPLORING

Inspired to learn more? Here are some more women photographers to research!

Letizia Battaglia: Brave Italian photojournalist and photographer.

Lola Álvarez Bravo: The first ever Mexican female photographer!

Karimeh Abbud: First woman photographer in the Arab world.

Homai Vyarawalla: India's first woman photojournalist.

Claude Cahun: French surrealist photographer, sculptor, and writer.

Ami Vitale: Photographer for *National Geographic* and author of the book *Panda Love*, featuring photos of the animals in the wild.

Shirley Baker: Pioneering British street photographer.

Abigail Heyman: Groundbreaking feminist photojournalist.

Graciela Iturbide: Mexican photographer known for her black-and-white images of indigenous people in her country.

Tina Modotti: Italian American photographer, model, actor, and political activist.

Zaida Ben-Yusuf: Portrait photographer named as one of the "Foremost Women Photographers in America" in 1901.

Jessie Tarbox Beals: One of the first published female photojournalists in the United States and the first female night photographer.

ABOUT THE CREATORS

THE ILLUSTRATOR

From a young age, **Vanessa Perez** knew she had a connection with art and telling stories through drawings. This love for creating led her to pursue a career in illustration. Since graduating with a Bachelor of Fine Arts in Illustration from California State University Long Beach, Vanessa has been working as a freelance illustrator, creating drawings for individuals and small businesses. She primarily works digitally and occasionally with gouache paint. Vanessa is a Southern California native and loves exploring new food creations, roller skating at the beach, and spending time with friends and family.

THE AUTHOR

Darcy Reed is a writer, editor, actor, and pop culture junkie. Her other projects include: Photography Trivia Deck, *Captain Marvel: The Tiny Book of Earth's Mightiest Hero*, *The College Bucket List*, *The Tiny Book of Jane Austen*, and *William Shakespeare: Famous Last Words*. She lives in Sonoma County, CA.